WHEN CAN I COME HOME?

Louise and Richard Spilsbury

www.raintreepublishers.co.uk
Visit our website to find out more information about **Raintree** books.

To order:
☎ Phone 44 (0) 1865 888112
▤ Send a fax to 44 (0) 1865 314091
▭ Visit the Raintree bookshop at **www.raintreepublishers.co.uk** to browse our catalogue and order online.

First published in Great Britain by Raintree, Halley Court, Jordan Hill, Oxford OX2 8EJ, part of Pearson Education.

Raintree is a registered trademark of Pearson Education Ltd.

Editorial: Louise Galpine, Harriet Milles, and
           Rachel Howells
Design: Richard Parker and Tinstar Design
           www.tinstar.co.uk
Illustrations: International Mapping
Picture Research: Hannah Taylor
Production: Alison Parsons
Originated by Modern Age
Printed and bound in China by Leo Paper Group

ISBN 978 1 4062 0846 7 (hardback)
ISBN 978 1 4062 0854 2 (paperback)
12 11 10 09 08
10 9 8 7 6 5 4 3 2

British Library Cataloguing in Publication Data
Spilsbury, Louise
When can I come home? - (Fusion history)
1. World War, 1939-1945 - Children - Great Britain
- Juvenile literature 2. World War, 1939-1945
- Evacuation of civilians - Great Britain - Juvenile
literature
I. Title II. Spilsbury, Richard, 1963-
940.5'3161'0941
A full catalogue record for this book is available from the British Library

Acknowledgements
The publishers would like to thank the following for permission to reproduce photographs: The Art Archive pp. **23** inset (Eileen Tweedy), **28** (Culver Pictures); Corbis pp. **7**, **9**, **15** main, **17**, **19**, **21**, **27** (Hulton-Deutsch Collection), **12** (Bettmann); Getty Images pp. **11** (Keystone), **13** (Fox Photos), **23** (London Express), **25** (Central Press); TopFoto pp. **5** (Roger Viollet), **15** top (HIP/The National Archives).

Cover photograph of bomb-wrecked houses in Coventry reproduced with permission of Corbis/Hulton-Deustch Collection.

Every effort has been made to contact copyright holders of any material reproduced in this book. Any omissions will be rectified in subsequent printings if notice is given to the publishers.

The publishers would like to thank Bill Mariott and Lynne Bold for their assistance with the preparation of this book.

Disclaimer
All the Internet addresses (URLs) given in this book were valid at the time of going to press. However, due to the dynamic nature of the Internet, some addresses may have changed, or sites may have changed or ceased to exist since publication. While the author and publishers regret any inconvenience this may cause readers, no responsibility for any such changes can be accepted by either the author or the publishers.

It is recommended that adults supervise children on the Internet.

Contents

Some words are printed in bold, **like this**. You can find out what they mean on page 30. You can also look in the box at the bottom of the page where they first appear.

Evacuation

Great Britain went to war against Germany on 3 September 1939. The German leader Hitler had just invaded Poland. From September 1940 **air raids** began. German planes dropped bombs on British cities. The bombs destroyed homes. Thousands of people were killed.

Thousands of city children were sent to safe places in the countryside. This was called **evacuation**. Their parents stayed in the cities to carry on working. We can tell from their letters home that many children were very homesick. The letters in this book are from an imaginary boy to his parents during World War II. They show what evacuation might have been like.

World War II

World War II was fought between 1939 and 1945. It is called a world war because it involved many countries. Great Britain, the Soviet Union, America, and Australia were known as "the Allies". The Allies fought against Germany, Italy, and Japan.

air raid attack by enemy planes
evacuation when people move from a dangerous place to somewhere safe

German planes bombed British cities. They wanted to scare British people. They hoped that the people would ask the British government to give in. The Germans also wanted to destroy British factories and shipyards.

Orchard Farm
South Devon
5 September 1940

Dear Mum and Dad,

I can't believe I'm here in Devon. It was only yesterday that you left me at the station. They pinned a label to my jacket. They wanted to make sure I didn't get lost. It made me feel like a piece of luggage! I sang songs with some other children to keep cheerful. Some of the little ones thought they had been sent away for being naughty. They cried and cried.

I saw so much from the train window. I had never seen cows before. There were so many fields and trees. Not like London at all.

A man called a **billeting officer** met us off the train. He took us round the village. He gave each of us to different families. I'm living with a farmer and his wife. They seem nice. But I don't know why you had to send me here. When can I come home?

Jim

6

billeting officer	person who finds homes for evacuated people
evacuee	person who has evacuated (left) a dangerous place
torpedoes	underwater bombs

Many **evacuee** children left by train. Some went to relatives, but many went to strangers. It was the first time most of these children had been away from home.

Evacuation overseas

In summer 1940, the British government **evacuated** nearly 3,000 more children. They were sent to Canada and other countries ruled by Britain. The scheme stopped when **torpedoes** from enemy submarines sunk one of the ships. Seventy-seven out of the ninety children on board died.

The Blitz

12 Church Street

London

25 September 1940

Dear Jim,

Dad and I were so happy to get your letter. I cried for hours after you left. But it's for the best. You would not be safe here. The bombing has been terrible. The **air raids** go on all night long.

They're calling the bombings the **Blitz**. That's short for "Blitzkrieg", which is German for "lightning war". It certainly looks like lightning when the bombs explode.

The most damaged homes are by the **docks**. The planes target the ships there. But lots of the bombs hit houses instead. All that's left of some streets is dust and bricks. I'm so glad you are safe in the country.

Keep smiling, son.

Mum

Blitz   period of intense bombing in Britain, from 1940–1941

docks   place where ships park and load or unload

Many people had to move out of the East End of London when their homes were destroyed by the bombs.

German bombers used the shape of the Thames River to find their targets in London.

Background to the bombs

At first the Blitz was just in London. From November 1940 to February 1941 the bombing spread to other British cities, such as Coventry and Liverpool. Like London, many of these places had docks. Others had factories making war planes or weapons. The map shows some of the worst-hit cities in Britain.

West End East End
City Docks
River Thames
GREATER LONDON
0   5 miles
0   5 kilometres

N
W E
S

ATLANTIC OCEAN

SCOTLAND

Glasgow

North Sea

NORTHERN IRELAND

IRELAND

Liverpool Manchester
Sheffield
ENGLAND

Birmingham Coventry
WALES

Bristol London

Southampton Portsmouth

Plymouth

English Channel

⊛ capital city
• other city
— modern day border
✴ bombed cities

0   50   100 miles
0   50   100 kilometres

9

Orchard Farm
South Devon
5 October 1940

Dear Mum and Dad,

Just a note to let you know I'm all right. The farmer and his wife are called Mr and Mrs Goodman. They are quite old but they are kind to me. I'm so glad I'm with them. My friend Bill says his host family smack him because he wets the bed. He's really homesick.

There is only one teacher at our school here. There aren't many books, so we have to share. We have to write on scrap paper too. There's not enough paper to go round. Some of the kids tease me because of the way I talk. But I think it's Devon voices that sound funny.

Today we tried using our **gas masks** again. I hate mine. It steams up. I can't breathe easily with it on. But I do like riding to school on the milk lorry. It picks me up after it has collected milk from the farm.

What do you do when the bombs come?

Jim

Safety plans

The British government gave everyone gas masks to use. They did this in case the Germans dropped poisonous gas. Children also had **air raid** drills at school. They practised putting on the masks and lying under their desks. This was to protect them from flying glass and splinters if a bomb hit their school.

↑ *Children were taught how to use their gas masks at school.*

A family sits outside the Anderson shelter that saved their lives during an air raid.

12 Church Street

London

30 October 1940

Dear Jim

I'm glad to hear you're going to school. The children who stayed here miss a lot of lessons because of the **air raids**. So think yourself lucky.

Don't worry about us. When the air raid **sirens** start wailing, your dad and I go into the **Anderson shelter**. It's made of sheets of metal and is half-buried in the back garden. It's small, damp, and dark in there. I read my magazines by candlelight. One night we were stuck inside it for eight hours!

At night we see the powerful beams of the searchlights. These are like giant torches. They scan the sky for bomber planes. When the lights show up a plane, guns on the ground fire at it. I don't think they hit many. But at least it feels like we're fighting back.

Be good.

Mum

Anderson shelter   metal hut that protected people from bombs
siren   loud sound that acts as a warning signal

Underground shelters

In the **Blitz** many people sheltered in the London Underground. People slept on station platforms. But it was not always safe. In 1940 a bomb went through a road near Balham station. It blew up water pipes. The water drowned 68 people who were sheltering there.

Underground stations were often crowded and uncomfortable, but people tried to keep cheerful.

Wartime food

Orchard Farm
South Devon
15 November 1940

Dear Mum and Dad,

For tea today we had a lovely rabbit pie and a blackberry and apple crumble. The food is nice here. There's always plenty of milk and vegetables. Most days we have eggs for breakfast. The one thing I don't like is raw turnip!

My job is to feed the hens and collect their eggs before school. Then I fetch the cows in the evenings. Mr Goodman has even taught me how to milk them.

Mr Goodman says farmers have to grow more food now. He's got some **land girls** working with him. They are planting lots of potatoes. Potatoes are cheap and they fill you up.

Write soon.

Jim

Land girls

In World War II, women did many of the jobs that men used to do. Women worked in factories. They drove ambulances, and did office work. In the countryside many worked in the Land Army. They did farm work, such as digging and ploughing.

land girls   young female farm workers in World War II

The need is 'GROWING'

DIG FOR VICTORY STILL

Government posters like this encouraged people to grow their own food.

12 Church Street

London

2 December 1940

Dear Jim,

I'm glad to hear you are eating well. Every day I queue at the shops to get food. I use the **coupons** in our **ration book** to buy things like butter, tea, and meat. There is not much fruit here, but we're growing vegetables in the garden.

We only get a little sugar. I made some carrot marmalade and fudge. It doesn't taste too bad. There isn't much meat either. But we have tried eating pigs' brains! The fish shop also sells whale meat. Dad doesn't like it. You are lucky to have fresh eggs every day. The dried egg we use makes food taste rubbery!

Fondest wishes,

Mum

→ *Each member of a family was given their own ration book. You had to look after your ration book very carefully.*

16

coupons tickets
ration book book of coupons used to claim a share of food or other goods
rationing dividing up a limited supply of something so everyone gets a fair share

When people bought food, they had to hand over a coupon from their ration book as well as the money.

Rationing

Food was scarce in the war. The German navy stopped ships bringing food into Britain. Ration books were given out to everybody. This was to make sure everyone got a fair share of the food available. For an adult, the weekly **ration** was:

- 56 g (2 oz) of butter

- between 56 and 225 g (between 2 and 8 oz) of cheese

- 115 g (4 oz) of margarine

- 1.7 litres (3 pints) of milk

- 1 fresh egg and 1 packet of dried eggs

- 56 g (2 oz) of tea

- 225 g (8 oz) of sugar

- 115 g (4 oz) of bacon

Christmas and blackouts

Orchard Farm
South Devon
28 December 1940

Dear Mum and Dad,

Thank you for the comic, toy warplane, and chocolate you sent for Christmas. I did feel homesick, but on Christmas Eve there was a party for **evacuees**. It was in the church hall. They played music and there were games. As a special treat we were each given an orange. It was my first orange for two years!

This morning we went to the cinema in town. It was packed with people. There was a film that showed our pilots fighting the Germans. Then we saw an American cowboy film.

Every night we all sit down to listen to the radio. Mr Goodman never misses the news. I like the comedy shows afterwards.

What have you been up to?

Jim

Many towns and villages held Christmas and New Year parties to cheer up evacuee children.

News and entertainment

There were no televisions in World War II. People heard the news at the cinema or from the radio. Comedy shows made fun of things like **rationing** and **gas masks**. The government wanted programmes like this to keep people cheerful.

12 Church Street

London

2 January 1941

Dear Jim,

We missed you a lot on Christmas day. But your dad and I managed a smile. Dad gave me two new bars of soap. That cheered me up. I gave Dad some gardening tools and some plant seeds.

Your dad was out a lot. He is an **ARP warden**. He has to check that everyone obeys the **blackout** rules. People must draw their curtains and turn off their lights when it gets dark. We don't want German planes to see us! Everywhere looked very dull at Christmas. There were no lights on the Christmas trees and no shop-window displays.

Dad still feels bad sometimes that he is not out fighting. But he can't be a soldier because of his weak heart.

Love,

Mum

This ARP warden is telling people where to go for help after an air raid.

ARP warden   person who helped to protect people during air raids

blackout   time when no lights were allowed to be seen outside

Blackout!

During the war it was important that enemy bombers did not see any lights on the ground. At night, doors and windows were covered with thick curtains. Streetlights were switched off. At night, vehicles had their headlights masked.

Wartime work

Orchard Farm
South Devon
15 February 1941

Dear Mum and Dad,

I'm doing my bit for the war effort! I've been collecting old metal pots and pans with my friends. We take them to the dump. Then they are melted down. They are used to make aircraft and weapons. When we see a British plane we smile at each other. Maybe it is made from the frying pans we collected!

Mrs Goodman makes me go to Sunday school at the church. This weekend the vicar took us on an outing. We went to the seaside. It was the first time some **evacuees** had ever seen sand or sea. There was barbed wire on the beach. It was to stop German boats landing. I wish you could have seen it.

From Jim

The government asked for a metal collection to help the war effort. This picture shows pans and a toy aeroplane, given by people from Chelsea.

Nazi   the name of Hitler's political party

The "squander bug"

During World War II the British government wanted to stop waste. It made posters to persuade people to help. Some showed a "squander bug" ("squander" means waste). The bug was covered in German **Nazi** symbols. The posters said that if you wasted things you were helping the enemy.

12 Church Street

London

10 April 1941

Dear Jim,

We have been busy here too. I'm now a **volunteer** with the **Women's Voluntary Service (WVS)**. This morning I helped some people. Their homes had been bombed during the night. We gave them blankets and tea. We tried to cheer them up. But it's very sad. They'll have to go to live with neighbours or relatives now.

The volunteer fire-fighters are the bravest. They are out every night. They fight fires caused by the bombs. The noise from the bombs keeps us awake at night. In the daytime everyone tries to carry on as normal. They get up and go to work. Workers on their way to the **docks** and the weapons factory look very tired.

Take care,

Mum

WVS women like these served tea to teams of workers from mobile canteens.

Homecoming

12 Church Street

London

May 1941

Dear Jim,

It's your dad writing this time. Your mum is too excited to sit still. The **Blitz** is over, son! It is time for you to come home.

Your mum is busy making you a new shirt from an old sheet. She's also cutting down a pair of my old trousers. She wants you to have something new to wear when you get home.

You will see that a lot has changed in London since you left. The roof of your old school was blown off. Lots of the houses have been flattened. Some are hanging in pieces. Everywhere is filthy and covered in dirt from the fires. But it will be good to be together again.

See you soon,

Dad

Evacuees return to London after the Blitz. As well as children, old people, pregnant women, and disabled people had been evacuated during the war.

End of the Blitz

The Blitz on Britain ended in May 1941. Hitler sent German warplanes to attack Russia instead. Some **evacuee** children went back home. But many did not return until the end of the war in 1945. Sadly, some children had no homes or families to go back to.

The Blitz in brief

During the **Blitz** (1940–1941) over 1 million houses were destroyed. Around 20,000 people were killed in London alone. During this stage of the war, more British women and children were killed by enemy bombs than British soldiers in battle.

German bombs fall around
St. Paul's Cathedral in 1940. ↓

Timeline

1940

7 September

The Blitz begins at around 4 p.m. Overnight 350 German planes bomb London.

18 September

Oxford Street is bombed.

15 October

Five railway stations are damaged.

2 November

This is the only day when there was no bombing, because of bad weather.

14 November

The centre of Coventry (including its cathedral) is destroyed.

29 December

Fire bombs cause over 1,400 fires in the City of London.

1941

11 January

Bank underground station is hit, killing 58 people.

6 February

Hitler orders his bombers to target ports in Plymouth, Portsmouth, Bristol, Swansea, and other major cities.

19 March

500 bombers target Docklands, killing 750 and injuring 1,000 people. The Port of London is the most bombed target in Britain.

19 April

More bombs are dropped on London than on any other night previously.

10 May

Last night of the Blitz: 1,500 are killed and 1,800 seriously injured. Parliament buildings are damaged.

Glossary

air raid attack by enemy planes. During an air raid many planes drop bombs on targets on the ground.

Anderson shelter metal hut that protected people from bombs. They were built in back gardens.

ARP warden person who helped to protect people during air raids. ARP stands for Air Raid Precautions.

billeting officer person who finds homes for evacuated people. They checked houses and decided how many children a family had room for.

blackout time when no lights were allowed to be seen outside. People turned off lights or used thick curtains.

Blitz period of intense bombing in Britain, from 1940–1941

coupons tickets. Ration book coupons proved you could have amounts of food.

docks place where ships park and load or unload. Enemies bombed ships.

evacuation when people move from a dangerous place to somewhere safe. During World War II children went to places that were unlikely to be bombed.

evacuee person who has evacuated (left) a dangerous place

gas mask mask to protect people from poisonous gas. Gas masks were worn over the face.

land girls young female farm workers in World War II. They worked in place of the men who had gone to war.

Nazi the name of Hitler's political party. Hitler's supporters were called Nazis.

ration book book of coupons used to claim a share of food or other goods. Shopkeepers took tokens from the books when they gave you the goods.

rationing dividing up a limited supply of something so everyone gets a fair share. During World War II, food, fuel, and other things were rationed.

siren loud sound that acts as a warning signal. During the Blitz sirens warned of air raids.

torpedo underwater bomb

volunteer someone who does a job without being paid. During World War II, volunteers helped in many ways.

Women's Voluntary Service (WVS) women who helped others after an air raid. They gave hot drinks and food to firemen and rescue workers, and first aid and comfort to victims.

Want to know more?

Books to read

Evacuation (At Home in World War II), Stewart Ross (Evans Brothers Ltd, 2007)
This book uses diaries, posters, newspaper cuttings, and oral accounts to show what evacuation was really like.

The Blitz, Vince Cross (Scholastic, 2001)
Edie Benson is caught in the bombing of 1940 and evacuated to Wales with her brother. Read her story.

Websites

www.bbc.co.uk/history/british/britain_wwtwo/
On this website you can read information about World War II and the words of real-life evacuees remembering their ordeal.

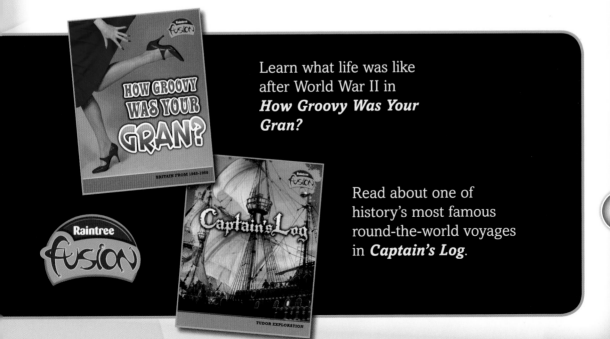

Learn what life was like after World War II in *How Groovy Was Your Gran?*

Read about one of history's most famous round-the-world voyages in *Captain's Log*.

Index